Written by Zoe Clarke

Illustrated by Xavi Ramiro

Meet Charlie and Ruby. They are best friends.
Hello!
Hi!
Charlie likes fixing things.
Squeak!
Clang!
Mechanic at work.
Ruby likes mixing things.
Splat!
Squelch!
Chemist at work.

They go to Lodge Village School, where Charlie tries to fix things …
My chair!

… and Ruby tries to mix things.
My paints!

Their fixing and mixing puts Mr Swinson in a rage!
Headteacher

Every year, there's an exciting contest at Lodge Village School.
INVENT A MACHINE
WIN THE LODGE CUP!
The Lodge Cup could be ours …
We just need to invent a fantastic machine!

Charlie and Ruby hid behind a hedge to see what the other teams were up to.

That weekend, Ruby and Charlie spent ages drawing pages of plans.
Technical plans
At last, they had a winning design.
CHAOS MACHINE
Then, they looked in a robotics brochure, but …
Everything costs too much money!

So, Charlie barged around and found some wires and cogs.

Ruby found some paint next to the fridge.

After much fixing and mixing … and with a little help from Charlie's big brother …

It was the day of the contest. There were three machines for the judges to look at.

And what can a chaos machine do?
THE CHAOS MACHINE
We're not quite sure ...
... but let's give it a go! Ready?
CLICK!
Nothing happened.
Well, for once you haven't created chaos!

Did you put the batteries in?
Silly me.
Ruby pressed the green button again. The chaos machine started.
HUMMMM
Charlie pressed the blue button. Lights on the chaos machine flashed.

A bolt of light exploded from the machine and hit Mr Swinson's dog.
ZAP!
The dog started to shrink. He got smaller and smaller ...
Nigel!
... and smaller.
Oops.

We're just having some technical problems.
Click!
ZAP!
Light exploded out again.
Mr Swinson got smaller and smaller. Ruby and Charlie winced.
Change me back!

ZAP!
ZAP!
No need to panic! Let's put them all in this budgie cage.
Charlie looked at the pages of plans for the chaos machine.
Let's mix up the cogs.

Ruby mixed up the cogs.
Charlie pressed the green and blue buttons. The lights flashed.
ZAP!
The light hit a spider on the window ledge. It grew bigger.

That is one giant arachnid!
A what?
Now was not the time for tricky words ...
It's a massive spider!
I've got the machine.
I've got the cage.
Everyone made a run for it.

Ruby and Charlie jumped on to the stage.
Make me bigger!
ZAP!
Charlie got bigger and bigger.
I'm huge!
He trapped the spider under a large crate.
Got you!
SLAM!

Ruby let everyone out of the cage and zapped them bigger.
ZAP!

Then, she mixed the machine's cogs once again and zapped Charlie and the spider smaller.
ZAP!

Later, at the prize-giving ceremony …
Do you think we won?
I think it's close!
The winners of the Lodge Cup are …
… the fudge machine and the badge machine!

But … but, we created chaos!
The judges really don't like chaos.
We liked the chaos.
But we liked the spider smaller!
We can make another machine next year!
CHAOS 2

You should have won, too.
We can share the Lodge Cup with you.
If I make some fudge, can you zap it bigger?
Stand back!
SPLAT!

I've made you badges!
We can zap them bigger, too.
Chaos
Chaos
We have fudge, badges *and* the Lodge Cup!
And we didn't even press the red button.
Chaos
CLICK!
BANG!
Oops!

Phonics Practice

Say the sound and read the words.

/k/	ch

school arachnid headache character

/sh/	ch

chef machine chiffon brochure

/j/	-ge

page barge ages village cabbage

/j/	-dge

bridge fridge hedge fudge ledge

Can you say your own sentences using some of the words on these pages?

What other words do you know that are spelled in these ways?

/u/	o

brother mother won other another

Common exception words

where many again thought through

We may say some words differently because of our accent.

Talk about the story

Answer the questions:

1 What was the name of Ruby and Charlie's school?

2 Why couldn't the children buy the things they needed to build their machine?

3 What happened to Nigel the dog when Charlie pressed the blue button?

4 Why did the winners of the Lodge Cup share it with Ruby and Charlie?

5 If you could invent any kind of machine, what would it do?

6 What kind of contest would you like to take part in?

Can you retell the story in your own words?